Mess Into Masterpiece

By Brett Gilford

Mess Into Masterpiece
by:
Brett Gilford

Copyright 2025 iCHAMPION Publishing

All right reserved. No portion of this book may be reproduced, scanned, stored in a retrieval system, transmitted in any form or by any means- electronically, mechanically, photocopy, recording or any other- except for brief quotations in printed reviews, without written permission of the publisher. Please do not participate or encourage piracy or copyrighted materials in violation of the author's rights. Purchase only authorized editions.

Published by iCHAMPION Publishing
P.O. Box 2352 Frisco, TX 75034

Content edit by Nikia Hammonds-Blakely and iCHAMPION Publishing

Library of Congress Cataloging-in-Publication Data Publisher and Printing by

iCHAMPION Publishing
© Copyright 2025 iCHAMPION Publishing

Written By: Brett Gilford
Cover Design By: iCHAMPION Publishing

ISBN: 9798264464515

Books › Biographies & Memoirs › Memoirs [↗]
Books › Self-Help › Self-Esteem [↗]
Books › Religion & Spirituality › Christian Books & Bibles › General [↗]

Dedication

To my Lord and Savior Jesus Christ for saving me, for without you, none of this would be possible.

To my loving wife Doris and our children. Thank you for your love and support! It has, and continues to be, the wind beneath my wings as I walk through this world holding hands with my Savior.

To Ginger, my therapist and lifelong friend. I couldn't have gotten to this point without God, working through you, to help clean up the mess that was my life.

To all of the 12 Steppers out there, "Keep coming back, it works if you work it".

To the January's, the impact you have had on my life can't be measured or articulated without me shedding tears. I am grateful to God for the day He allowed our paths to cross.

To Cheryl and Evelyn, keep Resting in His Word and you'll be Empowered with Joy while Walking in the Word.

To my Bridge of Frisco family, keep connecting the heart of God to the hearts of men.

Special Thanks

To Dr. Nikia Hammonds-Blakely and the iCHAMPION Publishing team. It has been a real joy. Thank you for being the midwife to this project.

Contents

Chapter 1: The Voice That Saved Me 1

Chapter 2: From Brokenness to Breakthrough 9

Chapter 3: The People Who Shaped Me 22

Chapter 4: The Making of a Testimony 29

Chapter 5: The Process of Recovery 38

Summary 46

Prayer of Repentance & Transfomation 48

CHAPTER 1
The Voice That Saved Me

And after the earthquake a fire; but the Lord was not in the fire; and after the fire a still small voice.

— I King 19:12 KJV

This book is going to start off differently than most. My life is a testament of the goodness of the Lord. It wasn't pretty, yet God protected me.

Growing up, I experienced things no child ever should. Yet, he was with me, and I understand that it was necessary to bring me to where I am now.

I've been able to share the dark side of life with others; that even though it may have seemed as though God was not there, He was, and that's the only reason why I did not die in it!

It made me who I am. I have wisdom and insight as a result, and can minister to others that are in need of light while they are in the midst of their darkness.

The voice of God.

I was an original crack head. When I started smoking cocaine it was called free base. My addiction started when they made it affordable by selling it in pieces.

I recall one Saturday morning, in September 1984, I hadn't been to sleep since I got up to go to work the day before, which was payday. I was broke, had to be to work in a couple of hours, wanted some more dope and didn't get paid for another two weeks. I felt so hopeless, and I sat on the side of my bed with my pistol in my hand. I wanted to blow my brains out, but the voice that told me not to do it was louder than the one that told me to. And that's the voice I listen to today. To me, that was the voice of God. In the summer of 1984, I had another encounter with God. During that time, the post office stations hosted softball games, and the only reason I went was because they drank afterward. This particular day, there was a carrier from another station named Ray. He was an older guy, and I remember him sharing with me this one thing, he said "Youngblood, step outside yourself, look at yourself and then ask yourself, do you like what you see." I remember one morning waking up looking in the mirror, with bloodshot eyes, and I heard his voice. It wasn't too long afterwards, in October 1984, that I checked into treatment at Samaritan hospital for the first time.

Genesis

I was born in Detroit in 1957. The oldest of two boys. I had a younger brother, Stacey, who passed away in 1999 from AIDS related complications.

My parents were Charles and Marlan (MacNeal) Gilford. I was the first grandchild on my father's side of the family and oldest grandson on my mother's side.

We moved to Sorrento Street, somewhere around 1963/64 after President Kennedy was killed. I didn't realize it at the time, but Sorento Street was in an affluent Jewish neighborhood and our neighbors were Jewish as well. The bakery on the corner was Jewish, the owners of the house we bought from were Jewish. We had a Mezuhah on the door post that they left. It was a full Jewish neighborhood. Over time, it transitioned into an upper middle class black neighborhood. Growing up, my best friend was Clarence Franklin, Aretha Franklin's son. Willie Horton, one of the Detroit Tigers, lived on the next street and Marvin Gaye stayed two streets over. Berry Gordy's parents lived on the corner where I walked to school and I went to school with Berry Gordy's nephews, so that whole neighborhood was affluent. Thinking back, it was a good life and I realize how much my father sacrificed for us, as he worked two jobs to provide. My mother worked as a nurse (LPN) and later became an RN. On the weekends, I would stay at Brett Smith's house when my parents had to work, and I think my brother stayed with my grandmother. Brett's dad, Bill, and his brother David, along with my parents, grew up together as kids on the same street on the east side.

While I recognize the good that happened, throughout those years, there were also some traumatic moments that were the catalyst for my addiction. Being sexually abused by a friend of the family and then being physically abused by my mother.

Our childhood traumas caused my brother and I to miss a lot of school. For example, I lost out on a lot of the 5th grade, and my brother had to repeat the 1st grade. There was so much dysfunction in the house, that was the only way something like that could've happened. Even as I write this book, I'm still working through a lot of my mommy issues. While my dad was at work, there were different "uncles" that came over.

The person who had the most impact on my life was the one who eventually became her husband. He was my mother's friend's fiancé. I remember the first time I saw him was when my father gave my mother a surprise birthday party, and he was the one that brought her to the house. He would come over in the evenings, while my dad was at work. He used to have a gun with him that he would put on a table, which was fascinating to me, as a young boy.

Today, I wonder what he would have done had my father come home early. At this time in my parents' marriage, they were sleeping in separate rooms. My father was in the bedroom and my mother was in the den right across the hall from their bedroom. I don't know what happened, that was just how things were. I remember hearing my father tell my grandfather one night (after they split and I went to go live with him) when he thought I was asleep, that my mother pulled a gun on him once when they were still together.

The night my dad left.

One night, my father had my uncle pick him up from the house. He saw me, as I cried, watching him leave. That Friday, he picked us up from school and took us over to my grandfather's house. A day or so later, my mother picked us up from grandpa's house and took us over to her boyfriend's apartment on Ewald Circle. How we got to school I can't remember but I think we caught the city bus home. I don't remember how long I stayed there but it wasn't long.

My first time visiting my father, after they separated, the song "ABC" by the Jackson 5 was out, and I mentioned that I was going to ask my father to purchase it. My mother's boyfriend was very vocal about my dad not being able to buy me the album, because he couldn't afford it. But once I told my dad I wanted it, he bought it for me and we listened to it all weekend. When we returned to the apartment, my brother and I were taking a bath. I remember splashing water on his face and he cried, which pissed her boyfriend off. I don't remember if I was punished or not but I must have been because I told them I wanted to go live with my father. I was very adamant about it. The next day after school, my grandfather picked me up and took me to his house on the east side which is where my father was living along with one of my uncles.

I caught the bus to school every day. My grandfather would take me to the bus stop by Wayne State University, where the Hamilton bus picked me up and took me to Seven Mile and Meyers. I would walk to school from there. In the afternoon I would catch the same bus back home. It would take me to where I transfer and catch the crosstown bus the rest of the way home. Sometimes I would go all the way downtown and catch the E Warren bus in front of Crowley's department store to get home. I did this for the remainder of the 7th grade and the entire 8th grade. During the time, before my parents broke up, I was introduced to sex by the next-door neighbor girl who was babysitting us. She let me play with her breast. I had to be around 7 years old. Around that same time, my father's friend came into the picture. We had gotten our dog Candy, a black French poodle, from his mom. He sexually abused me for years. Sometimes he would babysit us, and then we'd go over to his apartment. He also would pick me up and watch car races. He never penetrated me; he just played with me and showed me what sperm looked like and said we were only doing this because we didn't have any girls present. He was clearly a pedophile. I remember once he got married to a young girl, we had a threesome. This all ended when I turned 14 and returned home from Campion. Unfortunately, he sexually abused my brother as well, being that he lived in the same neighborhood as my mom. I honestly think that is why my brother was gay. I believe because my first introduction to sex was from the girl next door that is why I was not gay, yet identifying my sexuality was challenging and we'll look at it later.

One thing I want to point out as I mentioned earlier is that kids are not resilient as some people believe, and I deal with abandonment and other mother issues today.

CHAPTER 2

From Brokenness to Breakthrough

"For I will restore health to you, and I will heal your wounds, says the Lord, because they have called you an outcast, saying, This is Zion, whom no one seeks after and for whom no one cares!"

— **Jeremiah 30:17 AMPC**

After graduating from elementary school in 1971, my dad sent me to this prestigious Catholic high school, named Campion, an all boys college prep school, in Prairie du Chien, Wisconsin where I started 9th grade. That's where I started smoking cigarettes and was introduced to alcohol and weed. My roommate brought two fifths of Canadian club whiskey back from spring break and we got drunk. Not too long after that we got caught twice, with girls in the dorm, my roommate and I were asked not to return back to school.

After coming back home, I hung out with some guys in the neighborhood and a group of us became real tight. We hung out just about every day, hustling little jobs around the neighborhood and getting high together. For a time, I used to wash and detail cars in my driveway. Delores, who lived across the street from us, taught me how to clean and detail cars. She used to babysit me when I was a little boy, and was one of Uncle Stanley's old girlfriend's. In those days, we didn't have vacuums, so we used a whisk broom to clean the floors of a car. I had one steady customer, who lived down the street, Mrs. Merriweather. She had a black, 4-door Buick 225. I would wash her car every week so she could go to church in a clean car.

My grandfather, Dan, had a very strong impact on me had a very strong impact on me that didn't manifest itself until I got saved, clean and sober. I remember as a kid, he and I going grocery shopping on Saturday mornings at the Chene and Ferry market to get produce. He taught me how to take care of the yard, iron clothes and basic minor tasks around the house. He really loved me and now I can see God loving me through him. He told me that he didn't have a lot of book knowledge, he had fireside training and, unbeknownst to me, he passed that wisdom onto me. I later learned that my grandmother taught him how to read. I remember at night before he went to bed, he would be sitting in his room reading a little red book of Bible verses and he would sometimes ask me what certain words were. He was a good man.

My grandmother passed away in 1969 and, as a kid she really loved and spoiled me; being that I was the first grandchild. I loved her so much. Hindsight being 20/20 vision, I see how she was the glue that held our family together and when she passed, it seemed like all the marriages in the family eventually died too.

I graduated from East Catholic High School in 1975. Suffice it to say my alcohol and drug use escalated.

My beloved grandfather, Dan, died in May of 1976. I was drinking and doing drugs and never really grieved him. Even now, there are times when I wish I could talk to him because I miss him so much.

After high school, I attended Highland Park Community College for one semester. That's where I met the lady who eventually became my second wife and Matthew's (my son) mother. She and I went out to lunch, exchanged numbers and I never saw her again until 1990 at the post office where I was supervising. I was in the lobby, and recognized her. When I approached her, she was shocked at first because she thought I was a former prisoner; as she was a correctional officer at one of the prisons in the area. We'll talk more about that later.

Around Christmas 1975, my grandma Gertrude, on my mother's side, passed away. Not too long after that, in 1976, my grandfather went into the hospital and never came home.

I had my first job working at the main post office for the 1975 Christmas holiday. In April of 1976, I got hired again at the post office due to the UPS strike.

After that, I hustled painting houses and different odd jobs around the neighborhood. My best friend had a cousin that just got a job at this place called Standard Lead. It was a recycling center / scrap yard on the west side. I got hired and worked there, and at a neighborhood party store on E Warren until somewhere around 1978.

My dad remarried in July of 1977, and we remained in the house on the east side. During that same time, my home boys and I started going to a club every Thursday night in Toledo, Ohio called The Touch of Class. I met two ladies and, simultaneously, dated both. I'd have one come up to Detroit on one weekend, and the other lady on another weekend, or I would go down there. They both eventually got pregnant and in 1978, one gave birth to a baby girl, and the other a boy (we eventually found out that I wasn't his father). In 1976-77, I hung out with Tiger Dan, the radio disc jockey, doing gigs around the city in different venues. I became a club DJ and eventually my best friend Patrick, and another friend named JT and I started producing our own parties under the name 3 Wise Men Productions. We had a pretty good following as we hosted parties in the Ypsilanti, Belleville area and in Detroit. I had just started working at the post office in August of 1978. My main gig, as a DJ, was in this club called Point East on E. Warren and Chalmers where I met a young lady, moved out of my parents house and moved in with her. I bought a house, we broke up, and she moved out.

I had a few relationships after that, then I met my first wife. She was a sweet girl that I loved, and she really loved me, but she deserved better than I treated her. She was the bank teller where I cashed my check. Things moved quickly between us. We went out a few times, started living together and got married in 1983. It was at this time that my addiction took off. I was unfaithful to her, as I was in a relationship with a lady on my route who eventually became pregnant. She stuck by me through thick and thin. I found out years later through an extensive amount of therapy, and from a lot of relationships that I had with women, (some toxic), that I had walls and a defense system built up where I couldn't let them get too close or rather allow myself to be abandoned, like my mother did. We divorced in 1988. After going through a few toxic relationships, there was this girl I really liked. We dated for a few months. I really thought we had something, but she cheated on me with an old boyfriend of hers and we broke up. She really hurt me. A couple of years later, in 1990, Matthew's mother and I started seeing each other. We started living together, got married and had a baby.

In the fall of 1996, I went to training with the post office in Oklahoma and when I came home she had moved out of our bedroom and into the spare bedroom across the hall. Looking back, there were episodes where she would always say people were talking about her. Little incidents like this were occurring frequently. When she moved out of our bedroom, she thought I had someone in the house with me because our stairs creaked when I went up and down them. It got to the point where she hid my keys so I couldn't leave the house. We had deadbolt locks and we always left keys in them in case of an emergency. I tried to tell her sister that something was wrong but it fell on deaf ears. My father told me she didn't believe me because that was her sister and she and I were not getting along. One Sunday, while my wife was at work, her 14 year old son and I had words, where he cussed at me. One thing led to another and it got physical. I left with Matt and went to my mom's house. We came back to the house and she and her brothers were there. They told my mom and I to get my s**t and get out or get f***d up so I left and ended up sleeping on my mothers couch in the den. She went and got a restraining order against me. She told them I said I would kill her if she left me. This supposedly happened while we were having sex one time. I was reduced to seeing Matthew every other Saturday for three hours and my mother had to pick him up at the McDonald's restaurant. The first time I got to spend time with him, I cried. I was Matthew's main caregiver. I dropped him off at the daycare. When he was an infant, I took him to most of his doctor appointments. I made his bottles etc. It cost me two hundred dollars to get that restraining order lifted off of me, and in 1997 that was a lot of money.

I developed an intimate relationship with a woman that I used to work with. We became each other's nurse. Her dad was living with her as he had been diagnosed with prostate cancer. I helped her with him. I didn't realize until later how much she cared for me. I knew that I couldn't afford to take care of her. She had a beautiful 4k sq ft house in an affluent neighborhood. We talked about it years later and she said we could have done it together. I didn't know or see that.

I had some baggage from my childhood that affected my relationships with women.

As I said before, children are not as resilient as people think they are. That stuff shows up down the road.

They have scars; Some heal and some don't. They are lifelong hidden memories that manifest themselves in various ways- sometimes in self destructive behaviors. It's a built-in self defense system.

Walking with God provides healing. It's a process. Little by little the healing process takes place. The change is gradual and subtle. It might hurt a little and it's definitely going to be uncomfortable but you're striving towards a new normal. I trust God because I don't want to go back to the life of being on drugs. The only reason I ever look back is just to see how far He has brought me. I'm excited to see what He's got in store for me, ahead.

My move to Texas

This was truly a God thing.

In 1998 I was praying and the Spirit told me to "get ready to move". I brushed it off but it didn't go away. So I surrendered. I figured the Lord was telling me to get out of there before the place caught on fire or something. I told Him I wanted to be close to Matt and my church. So I rode around looking for a new apartment but nothing moved me.

Carl had just got promoted to Dallas and came back to finish up his move. They invited several of us out to dinner and afterwards, he and I just talked. He asked me what did I want, job wise, and that there was an open Manager position in Plano. He encouraged me to pray about it. As soon as I left the restaurant, I said "TEXAS, Lord?!" And I heard the Lord say "Yes, Confer not with flesh and blood". (The phrase "confer not with flesh and blood" comes from the Bible, specifically [Galatians 1:16](), and means to not seek advice or validation from other humans immediately after a divine calling or revelation.) After I applied for the job, and put everything in motion, I felt released to share the news with my in-home bible fellowship group. It was met with concern and sadness. They expressed how much they would miss me. As I walked to the car, the Lord spoke to me and said "That's why I told you not to confer with flesh and blood." In my experience, most people are well-intentioned when they offer you their advice. But when God gives you specific instructions, it's best for you to listen to Him. And that's exactly what I did.

In March of 1999, I got recruited to transfer with the post office to Dallas. All I had to do was get a ride to the airport. God took care of everything else. Part of the relocation process was a moving company packed everything in my apartment and put it on a moving truck, along with my car that was leaking oil, and shipped it all to Texas.

When I left Detroit I was paying 800 dollars a month in child support and learning how to tithe. All I wanted was a 2 bedroom apartment and a corvette. The relocation company put me in touch with a mortgage company and I was pre approved for a $80,000 mortgage. It didn't really hit me until I got here.

When I was in Detroit paying child support, car note and 300 dollars a month for rent I was struggling yet I kept serving God and stayed in the Word. I would be out doing route inspections and would see houses for sale and thinking "I'll never be able to afford another house." But God had a plan.

I went looking for houses and got led to a city called Little Elm where this developer was breaking ground. I gave my earnest money and cried while driving back to work. I was building a house.

I couldn't believe that this was happening and God was doing this for me. I was overwhelmed with emotions.

I joined the Potters House church immediately after arriving here on Easter Sunday and began serving in the sound /production ministry that summer. It was truly a blessing serving under Bishop Jakes and I was placed in a position where I placed the lavaliere microphone on him twice every Sunday morning for several years. To be in the position he holds, he is one of the most gracious down to earth men I have ever met, who really loves his people.

My brother Stacey passed away a month after I moved here. He was in the hospital but not expected to die. I went to a basketball game that Monday night and was going to call him, but decided to call him the next morning. After my teleconference I called his room and there was no answer. The call went back to the operator who transferred me to the nurses station. The nurse said that he didn't have a good night, that he passed away. I was shocked because I knew my parents were unaware since no one called me.

So I was communicating from Texas to Detroit. I called my father at the school he was teaching and told his principal what happened and to let him know because I was now living in Texas. I called my mom at work and had her co-worker talk to her. I think my sister who worked in the same hospital with her had just talked to my cousin in California and was on her way to tell her.

Two years later, my mother was still grieving about him, so I went back to Detroit around his birthday to see her. I saw Matthew while there. After my move, he would come to Texas and stay with me for the summer. When I returned home his mother called me and said it was my turn to raise him. So I put the legal wheels in motion and that summer we exchanged custody of him and his hamster. I was now a single parent, just like my dad was with me.

CHAPTER 3

The People Who Shaped Me

"But the God of all grace, who hath called us unto his eternal glory by Christ Jesus, after that ye have suffered a while, make you perfect, stablish, strengthen, settle you."

— 1 Peter 5:10 KJV

When I got out of treatment in 1984, it was my mom that took me in. I lost my home because of my addiction. My father told me I couldn't move in with them, which was good, because I was still using drugs and it would have really affected his marriage with Ella. Tell you how God works. That loss of my home never showed up on my credit report!! By the time I got out of treatment the second time, in 1985, I forgave my mom. I realized we were both just living our lives the best we knew how. When my second marriage ended, she helped me put the pieces of my life back together. When I moved to Texas I flew her down here and also took her on vacations with us and the kids to Florida.

My relationship with my first wife.

I did her wrong and I made my amends to her before I left Detroit. She deserved better and I'm happy to know that at this time she has been happily married for over 20 years. God blessed her with the right man.

My second wife.

We met in college and reconnected at the post office like I mentioned earlier. I really loved her and thought it would last forever. When things started to go sideways, I prayed for her with the prayers from a book by Germaine Copeland called "Prayers That Avail Much". It was when the marriage fell apart. I couldn't understand what happened, but I stayed faithful. I kept serving in church and kept praying and didn't lose my faith or hope in God. God answered my prayer with my current wife.

My current wife Doris.

God took me through a process of healing and getting into position spiritually, emotionally and mentally. After my subsequent move to Texas, I got involved with my church here and a few other fair relationships. I met my current wife and I knew she was the one, she was the answer to my prayer.

I have come to realize that my relationship with my mother affected my relationships with women. I was self destructive and didn't allow them to get too close emotionally because "they would leave", just like my mom did. I realized that my mother really loved me. I was blinded by my own feelings of the past.

Pastor Brady once said when it comes to our parents, our focus should be on their position, and not their performance.

My brother Carl.

God definitely knew what I needed and when I needed it when He allowed our paths to cross.

As my relationship with my second wife wasn't working out, he was there. I would call him every Sunday evening to talk. He really ministered to me at that time. After the move to Texas it grew even deeper to the point that we are brothers. He is one of my best friends. We talk at least once a week. We help each other through our struggles by getting God in our conversations. People always look to Him for guidance and encouragement.

My therapist Ginger.

She is, and continues to be a great friend, surrogate mother and sounding board. She was my out patient therapist in 1985 and through the years we built a relationship that not many patients and therapists enjoy. She has helped me through two divorces and the breakup of two toxic relationships that I almost interrupted my "clean time" over. God, working through Ginger, taught me the difference between being alone and being lonely. 1986 On my days off she had me go to the movies by myself. So I would go to the mall, get 3 cookies from Mrs Fields, popcorn and a drink and watch the movie. This was a valuable lesson because I am comfortable with Brett being alone. I don't need anyone to validate me. Another issue we resolved was my sexuality. I tell her that she took me through puberty with this one (she doesn't remember). I was attracted to men physically but not sexually and never approached them. Since my brother Stacey was gay she said go to a gay bar with him, so I did. While there I almost got into a fight with a woman over her girlfriend. That settled me not being gay.

Bill Broach.

He was my inpatient counselor both times I was a patient at Samaritan Hospital. He was one of my first sponsors and his wisdom and insight laid the foundation of my recovery.

Grandpa Dan Gilford.

I spent more one-on-one time with him than any of his children. He taught me a lot about life through his little sayings of wisdom that I carry with me to this day. People are always enlightened when I say one because they are timeless and appropriate. The two that come to mind: 1.)

You can lead a horse to water, but you can't make him drink. 2.) The best time to scald a hog is when the water is hot.

He was a no nonsense man. I miss him so much and I wish he could see the man I have become.

All of my Pastors.

Bishop Keith Butler got the ball rolling teaching the importance of getting into your Bible and spending time daily with God.

Bishop T.D. Jakes is an extremely gracious man who loves his people. Serving him and with him was an honor and a privilege. The wisdom that flows from him can't be matched.

Pastor Sheryl Brady loves her people so much and it shows. She's very compassionate and kind. I love her so much. God working through her has impacted not only my life but my entire family too. When she began Pastoring TPHND some of us came from Dallas to serve. Quite a few left and went back. I was working in production that just so happened to be in the area where she would come into the facility. At the time I was reading a book by Bishop I V Hilliard titled "The Cake Cup and the Coin". It was about honoring your spiritual leader. So every time I saw her I placed a seed in her hand. "A man's gift makes room for him and brings him before great men." Proverbs 18:16 AMPC. That's how we met and she knows me and my family well plus it doesn't hurt that we are both from Detroit.

CHAPTER 4

The Making of a Testimony

"Don't be afraid, for I am with you. Don't be discouraged, for I am your God. I will strengthen you and help you. I will hold you up with my victorious right hand."

— Isaiah 41:10 NLT

My Dad.

My dad was a good man. When my parents divorced I chose to live with him, and that was the best thing that could have happened to me at that point in my life. He and I had a great relationship that really blossomed as we both got older.

Ella was the love of his life, and he took care of her. He lived out his marriage vows with her. When she became sick with dementia, he made sure her hair and nails were regularly done. He kept her at home until he could no longer care for her, himself. While she was in the nursing home, he visited her every day he could. Even through the winter, driving through the snow from one side of town to the other. He was the example (that we continue to emulate) when it comes to walking out your marriage vows.

Dad & Ella traveled Europe and Asia together. He had a full life and the highlight of his life was his 4 grandchildren. Matthew (the first grandchild) was the apple of his eye that he loved and would go all out for.

When we became foster / adoptive parents he would come every year at Christmas time for a week to see them. When Ella passed - on his 80th birthday-he laid her to rest beautifully.

When he was diagnosed with cancer we moved him to Texas to be with us.

I saw him take care of his father until he passed, so he laid the foundation for me to do the same. After living with us for a while it became clear he needed his own place. Doris found a wonderful place for seniors. My wife furnished it and he loved it. The only thing we had to reconcile was his driving. He wanted a car but hadn't accepted the reality that he shouldn't be driving. Once we got past that point, he was okay. The apartment had a bus and took the residents grocery shopping and on outings to different places and events around town. I took him to all of his doctor appointments and to church on Sunday.

We had a lady come and clean the apartment, so basically he had everything he needed.

I jokingly tell people that the one thing I miss is being inconvenienced by him. We had countless memorable conversations on the drive to his cancer treatments. It was a great time of male bonding. There was a young brother who worked at the apartment complex and he looked out for him. When something happened and he went to the hospital, the guy called me and I went to the hospital to get him. The last time was on Ethan's birthday. I went to the emergency room and they took Dad to run some tests. He and I waited briefly for the results. The doctor came in and said that the cancer had spread to his brain. He was devastated. I could tell because he was always chatting in the car, but this time he was quiet and said he trusted God. Since it was Friday and Ethan's birthday, we always went out to dinner, so he came home with me and went out to eat and stayed the weekend. He periodically used a walker and when I took him home that Monday morning, he could barely walk. He called me that Wednesday afternoon and said goodbye. He had a good life and no regrets. I believe he was ready spiritually. We had hospice set up for him a couple of months prior to this episode. That Thursday the nurse called and said he couldn't get out of bed. We went over there and she said he didn't have much time left. That's the only time I cried. The nurses were angels in disguise. Sunday morning, a few minutes after my alarm went off to call him to get ready for church, the nurse called me and told me he passed. I went there and stayed with him until the funeral home came and picked him up. We had him cremated, as was his wish, and buried him with his Ella. I eulogized him at his church in Detroit. It was a beautiful service. Friends and family were there.

The first commandment with a promise is that we honor our parents and in doing so we will live long on the earth. My dad honored his father, and he outlived both of his parents, in age. Our children saw us take care of not only my dad, but Doris's mother also. When we had our current house built I had them widen her bedroom door so she could get her wheelchair in. I had modifications made so she could get in and out of the house without any issues to go to her dialysis appointments. She stayed with us until she passed.

My Children.

When we were dating, I told Doris that if having a baby was a deal breaker for her then she needed to find someone who would give her some babies, because I might not change my mind. She said it wasn't. After I retired, we completed classes to become foster parents. The first placement was a family of three, (two sisters and a brother). We were going out of town that weekend when they called us about them. We were told the children would be there when we got back. Normally, the state doesn't wait to place the children, but this time they did. The CPS worker said that all Trinity wanted was a dad. At only 4 years old this was her desire and guess what? It was fulfilled. She was the most traumatized of the 3 children. At the time, we had a dog named Jazz who immediately took to Trinity and basically became her dog. When the bus dropped her off from school, I had the door open and she would jump up and down when she saw Trinity coming.

Jasmine (8yrs old) was the quiet one who followed in Doris' footsteps and could really cook. Ethan (2yrs old) was my road dog. Since the girls were in school he hung out with me all day. There were times when we went to the YMCA. They had a place for children to play while parents were working out. On Tuesdays, we would go to Applebees because kids could eat for free. Ethan and I had a tight bond, and he was always very respectful. We had normal childhood issues with all of them, but we overcame them through the grace of God. It became clear that we were destined to be a family, so we made the prayerful decision to adopt them.

My Ministry.

While serving in the sound ministry at The Potters House, my team member, the late Elder/Prophetess Marva said I was going into the ministry. I said "Yeah, right". As it turned out, she was spot on. I enrolled in the school of ministry in 2007, became licensed in 2010, and was ordained as an elder in 2013. This was truly the hand of God and has been a blessing ever since I answered the call. In 2015, I published a book titled "5 Minutes with God", a 365-daily devotional that was birthed from the emails I sent to my friends. I was urged to put them in a book and I did. It has and continues to be a blessing to all who read it.

In 2010, my good friend Cheryl invited myself and another minister to join her radio show. That was the springboard to my digital ministerial presence. I owe a tremendous amount of gratitude to her. She taught me how to be radio-friendly and she groomed my broadcasting skills. We evolved from one Saturday a month, for one hour, to a weekly 2hour radio show, "Resting in His Word", heard every Monday around the world. Through a series of changes, we've had several people come and go on our team, yet she and I are still hanging in there. It has been 11 years strong. to God be the Glory! I do "5 Minutes with God" online every

Monday morning and a Bible study every Wednesday morning. Looks like Elder Marva really did hear from the Lord about me.

My Diagnosis.

After I moved to Texas, sometime during that summer, the left side of my torso felt numb. I thought I had slept wrong or something but it wasn't going away. I went to the doctor and they couldn't figure it out. Eventually it went away. Then, in early 2000, my eyes were bothering me and I couldn't see as well. I thought I needed new glasses, and I almost went blind. One day I drove to the corner and had to go right back home. I called my sister Marsha and she took me to the hospital and my subsequent appointments. After I had an MRI I received the results, it was MS. It had affected the contrast of my vision. Since there was no cure, I released my faith, went on with my life and was basically symptom free until 2006/7. I began taking treatments and physical therapy. The Word of God continues to strengthen me as I have incorporated a regimen of biblical confessions in the area of healing. I use the scripture verses that the late Dodie Osteen used, along with the scriptural confessions from the book by Charles Capps, "God's Creative Power for Healing". I'm still walking and regularly serving in the ministry at my local church, The Bridge Frisco. What I've learned from this and other physical challenges, is that I have to keep my focus on God's Word. I can't be moved by the way my body feels or any of the other stuff. I have to keep speaking the Word of God. The only thing I'm saying is what God says. I increase my faith daily in the Word. And you can do the same. God is no respecter of persons. If He did it for me, He'll do it for you.

My Miracle.

Labor Day 1985, I had a disagreement with a young lady. I was standing on the grass next to my car and she was on the sidewalk. We were about 10-20 feet apart when she pulled a gun out of her pocket. She chambered a round and pulled the trigger. It didn't fire so she repeated the process and it still didn't fire. She repeated it again and this time the gun fired. I got in my car and left. I don't know where that bullet went. It didn't go into my car or myself. I can only say that angels were on assignment and protected me, according to Psalms 91:11-12. I saw her several years later at a NA meeting where I was giving an open talk, and no words were ever spoken between us.

I shouldn't be here. But by the grace of God, I'm alive today.

CHAPTER 5

The Process of Recovery

"When the LORD turned again the captivity of Zion, We were like them that dream. Then was our mouth filled with laughter, And our tongue with singing: Then said they among the heathen, The LORD hath done great things for them."

— Psalm 126:1-2 KJV

The post office.

God took me, an alcoholic, crackhead, mailman and turned my life around. I tried to give them the job back. I really did. I was an attendance abuser. I called in (sick) all the time. I had been suspended at least four times for attendance and behavior. The last two suspensions were letters of removal, modified to a 21-day suspension both because of behavior. During the last suspension, I was 90 days clean and said some things about my supervisor. The thing about it was her husband was the manager of labor relations so they tied me up real nice and tight with corrective action. It was OK because I was already going to treatment. It was outpatient therapy, and I was going to Alcoholics Anonymous (AA) and Narcotics Anonymous (NA) meetings so they modified my letter of removal to a 21-day suspension and I had to go to the postal Employment

Assistance Program (EAP). It worked out. My manager told me to get my life together, get a hobby or something. He said he wasn't going to fire me but he was going to put my a$$ out there on Algonquin Street (and suspend me without pay -as many times as it takes to get the message). Then he asked me, didn't you just buy a new car? and I said yes. He said. "That's gonna be the first thing to go". He was convinced that if I didn't get my act together, my new car would be the first thing I would lose.

God turned things around and He took me from that position as a carrier and with the help of my managers, He placed me in management. I became a supervisor. I got recruited to Dallas, became a manager, and was detailed twice as an acting postmaster. They put me in charge of hundreds of thousands of dollars with the stamp stock, million dollar budgets with employees, vehicle & mail delivery responsibilities to hundreds of thousands of customers. I actually found my true niche in customer service.

I love helping people/customers. Something I learned when I was younger from John Bates when I worked at his neighborhood store. He said, "Brett, the customers don't need you, you need the customers and the customer is always right even when they are wrong because they're the customer". This principle has stayed with me my entire career. When I delivered mail, both in the hood on the east side of Detroit, to my route in Grosse Pointe Park, my customers loved me because I took great care of them. 30 years later, I'm still in touch with a few families from the Pointe. After I retired, I saw an ad that American Airlines was hiring customer service representatives, so I applied and was hired. That was the best job I've ever had. The atmosphere and the people were amazing.

Yet it went away with Covid, and to show you how God works, I took the offer of leaving and I accepted 33% of my pay and unemployment until the end of the year 2020. I also received 250,000 miles and 5 years of seniority. My actual 5 year seniority date was in November. So by that date, I had accumulated 10 years, plus my age made me eligible for retiree travel benefits- for life! We serve a good God and He's always looking out for us, making something good out of a bad situation. Thank You Jesus!

Since leaving treatment I interrupted my clean time twice; in November of 1985, and again in August of 1986, where I had recently celebrated 9 months clean. The last time was horrible. I couldn't understand how anyone who had been clean and used could stay out there. Head full of the program and dope don't mix. Here's what happened:

One Friday evening I went by an old girlfriend's grandmother's house, and her uncle was there. We never got high together and I didn't know he was in there smoking crack, but I walked in on him smoking, and I couldn't leave. With my hand on the doorknob, my mind told me to leave… but I sat down, trapped and tortured. I couldn't shut the program off in my head. Everything I would hear in those meetings played over and over in my mind, tormenting me. Those few hours changed my life. Afterwards, I wasn't going to tell anyone at the meetings what happened. Monday night I did. The guilt was so strong that I wanted to jump off the Belle Isle bridge into the Detroit river. I remember Mike asked me "Why didn't you call someone?" Through the grace of God I have been clean since and whenever I felt like using I called somebody. I needed that experience to be the foundation of my recovery. One of the old timers said "if you don't remember your last one, you haven't had it yet." I remember that day as if it were yesterday. One thing that helped me stay clean was getting actively involved in service work in Narcotics Anonymous. I started serving on the entertainment and fundraising committee, then I became a group rep for my home group, and eventually became the co-chair for the city of Detroit. I later became the first Detroit west area chair. I was the committee treasurer for DACNA1(the Detroit Area Convention of Narcotics Anonymous) and they are still going strong recently holding DACNA 32. There's a saying "We can only keep what we have by giving it away". Giving back and getting involved in spreading God's message of recovery is the foundation that helps me stay clean as I celebrate almost 40 years of uninterrupted clean time.

There were a couple of times when it got really tough, especially during the break up of the two toxic relationships I had, (both were in between my marriages, while I was still single). Ginger, my therapist, was there both times to help me get through it. The first time, I had almost 2 years clean time, and I thought I was in love. I really put myself out there and I was to blame for my own part of the breakup. The last time God moved my job assignment before it happened. I was temporarily assigned to the Addison post office as the postmaster. That was one of the best assignments I ever had. When everything went down there was an AA meeting right around the corner, everyday at noon. Here I was, 20 years clean, and an emotional wreck. There were a group of old white men there that helped nurse me back to health. I thank God for them. I needed both of those experiences to make me appreciate what I have today. The main thing I learned was how to treat people, and the consequences of the hurt I caused them by my actions. Getting your feelings hurt is not pretty and was a very valuable lesson for me to learn. I share that wisdom with my younger son who has recently discovered that there are girls he likes.

Right after that, my current wife Doris walked into my life. We met at church. I was in production and she was a pulpit usher, so our paths crossed frequently. When God introduced me to her I used to practice in the mirror how I was going to ask her out. I finally did. We met at the movies for our first date, and I fell asleep during the movie. We went to dinner afterwards so I redeemed myself. I would always call her in the mornings, never at night. She would say that I was different from the other guys. We dated and got married a year later on June 7, 2008 (6/7/8). How cool is that?! When my best man Carl drove me up to the wedding venue I cried. When I saw her coming to me, the tears were flowing. Her nephew was the ring bearer, and he asked me why I was crying and I told him I was so happy. At our wedding when I made my toast, I said after all the storms of my life, she was the pot of gold at the end of the rainbow. She still is… 17 years later, to this day.

Summary

"And Peter opened his mouth and said: Most certainly and thoroughly I now perceive and understand that God shows no partiality and is no respecter of persons,"

— Acts 10:34 AMPC

Mess Into a Masterpiece.

So, that's my story. The good, the bad and the ugly. Yet, through it all you witnessed the goodness of God in my life and how He transformed a mess into a masterpiece.

I've learned so much about the character of God and how He is faithful.

Through childhood trauma and abuse, both physically and sexually, I survived 13 solid years of an active addiction to alcohol and drugs, suicidal thoughts, being shot at, 2 failed marriages and 2 toxic relationships -that I almost interrupted my clean time over. As a result, I developed a relationship with my Heavenly Father through His Son Jesus Christ. I am continually growing in grace to become a better man, the man God created me to be. I am in the ministry, serving the people of God, and loving every minute of it. Today, I wouldn't change one thing I went through, because it made me who I am and most importantly I got to know God's love for me and I can share it with others. Through it all we both saw Him working it out. God can turn your life around and heal the broken, fractured parts in you. I'm a living witness. You just read how I let you behind the velvet rope of my life and see His hand at work. If He did it for me, He will do it for you too. He's no respecter of persons.

Prayer of Repentance & Transformation

Heavenly Father,

I come before You with a humble heart, acknowledging my sins, my failures, and the mess I've made along the way. I confess that I have fallen short of Your will and strayed from Your path. Forgive me, Lord, for every thought, word, and deed that has grieved Your heart. Wash me clean in the precious blood of Jesus.

Father, I surrender every broken piece of my life into Your hands. Where there is shame, bring Your grace. Where there is guilt, cover me with Your mercy. Where there is confusion, speak Your truth and bring clarity. I lay my burdens, regrets, and mistakes at Your feet, trusting that You are the God who makes all things new.

Lord, take my mess and turn it into a masterpiece — something that reflects Your glory. Use my story, even the painful parts, to show others the power of Your redeeming love. Mold me, shape me, and transform me into who You've called me to be. Let my life become a living testimony of Your faithfulness and grace.

I thank You, Father, for not giving up on me. Thank You for hearing my cry and pouring out Your unfailing love. I choose to walk in obedience, renewed purpose, and deeper intimacy with You. Have Your way in me, Lord. In Jesus' mighty name, **Amen.**

Made in the USA
Coppell, TX
15 December 2025

66004309R00031